COUNTRY CLUB
IT'S ALL ABOUT TO CHANGE

Cover Photography by Peter Nash

ISBN 0-7935-1022-8

7777 W. Bluemound Rd. P.O. Box 13819 Milwaukee, WI 53213

2

COUNTRY CLUB

IT'S ALL ABOUT TO CHANGE

From the very beginning, Travis Tritt has been a refreshingly different sort of country artist. His blend of honky tonk balladry, Southern Rock rowdiness, and melodic songwriting is as individual as it is easy to like. Tritt has proved his status as one of the country's fastest-rising talents with the certified platinum success of both his Warner Bros. debut album, *Country Club*, and his critically acclaimed second album, *It's All About To Change.*

Country Club, which yielded the three #1 singles "Help Me Hold On," "I'm Gonna Be Somebody," and "Drift Off To Dream," established Tritt as an artist of raw talent and unusual versatility. In fact, *Billboard* magazine named Tritt "Top New Male Artist" (Country) for 1990. Among the numerous other industry awards and nominations that the album garnered, *Performance* magazine named Tritt "Best New Country Act" for the same year.

He took his music to the next step with his follow-up album, *It's All About To Change.* Certified platinum within four months of its release, the album built upon the accomplishments of *Country Club* while extending Tritt's artistic reach still farther.

"We're trying to break down the barriers between different kinds of music," Tritt says. "I'm a firm believer that there only two kinds of music: good and bad. I like to describe my music as a triangle. On one side is a folk influence from people like James Taylor, Larry Gatlin, and John Denver. On the second side is George Jones and Merle Haggard — that type of music. And then on the third side is The Allman Brothers and The Marshall Tucker Band. They're all balanced together, all a part of what I do."

These diverse yet complementary elements can be heard on *It's All About To Change.* The first single from the album, "Here's A Quarter (Call Someone Who Cares)," is a stone traditional country ballad with a tongue-in-cheek edge. Songs like "Anymore" and "Someone For Me" (the latter featuring Tanya Tucker on backup vocals) display his grasp of contemporary country style. And Tritt asserts himself in a Southern Rock style with more energy than ever in songs that include "Bible Belt" and "Homesick."

It's All About To Change earned Tritt the prestigious Horizon Award from the Country Music Association, as well as two Grammy nominations for "Here's A Quarter (Call Someone Who Cares)" — for Best Country Song and Best Country Vocal Performance Male. In addition, *Music Row* magazine declared the video of "Anymore" to be "Video of the Year" for 1991.

Tritt describes his career as "overnight success that took eight and a half years to happen." Born and raised in Marietta, GA, he followed the classic country path by starting out as a soloist in the children's choir at the neighborhood church. Teaching himself guitar at the age of eight, he wrote his first song at 14.

Upon graduation from high school in 1981, Tritt went to work loading trucks and within four years had worked his way up to a position in management. Still, he continued to wonder if he had the talent to make it in country music. Not wanting to end up being someone who always believed he "could have been a contender," he quit his job and began playing solo at any club that would have him.

Tritt came to the attention of Danny Davenport, a local representative of Warner Bros. Records. At first, Davenport's interest in Tritt was simply as a writer, but once he began seeing him perform in front of an audience, he saw his potential as an artist as well. Together, at Davenport's home studio, they began working on an album. More than two years later, Davenport took the tapes to Warner Bros., which led to a singles and then an album recording commitment.

When Ken Kragen (best known as the manager of Kenny Rogers and organizer of "We Are The World") signed Tritt as his first entry-level act in more than 20 years, the winning team was complete. Tritt's first single, "Country Club," was released in November 1989 and reached #9 (*Billboard*) and #13 (*Radio & Records*). This was followed by "Help Me Hold On," which topped the charts in both publications. "I'm Gonna Be Somebody" (#2 *BB*, #1 *R&R*), "Put Some Drive In Your Country" (#28 *BB*, #20 *R&R*), and "Drift Off To Dream" (#3 *BB*, #1 *R&R*) kept Tritt's profile high on the charts. The first single off *It's All About To Change*, "Here's A Quarter (Call Someone Who Cares)," hit #1 in *BB* and #2 in *R&R*. Also from that album, "Anymore" and "The Whiskey Ain't Workin'" both hit #1 in *R&R*.

On the road, Tritt has confirmed his reputation as a dynamic live performer over and over again. Playing some 150 shows a year, he's developed a crowd-pleasing act that displays the full spectrum of his music. Perhaps a review by *The Milwaukee Journal* summed it up best: "Blunt as a two-by-four and twice as solid, Tritt commanded the crowd by force of presence." The review went on to say, "Tritt's performance, cutting any of his recordings to shreds, gave even the disc's weaker moments new life."

In addition to the critically acclaimed *It's All About To Change* album (produced by Gregg Brown, the man at the helm for *Country Club*), Tritt fans have a chance to see further sides of his life and music with the release of a 30-minute video of the same title. The tape, in addition to featuring song videos, includes backstage footage from concerts and recording sessions, as well as interviews with Tritt and his parents.

Tritt has said that the title *It's All About To Change* has a double meaning: in addition to being the name of a song on the album (about a relationship), it reflects his hopes that the album itself will be instrumental in establishing his career. But as far as his fans are concerned, the use of the future tense is unnecessary; with Tritt on the scene, things have already changed — for the better.

COUNTRY MUSIC HALL OF FAME
WALK OF FAME STAR PRESENTATION

PHOTO BY TIM CAMPBELL

TRAVIS TRITT FAN CLUB

P.O. BOX 440099

KENNESAW, GA 30144

COUNTRY CLUB

Words and Music by CATESBY JONES
and DENNIS LORD

I drive an old Ford pick-up truck; ___ I do my drink-in' from a

Dix - ie Cup. ___ I'm a bo - na fide danc - in' fool; ___

I shoot a might-y mean game of pool. ___ at an - y hon-ky-tonk or

road - side pub, ___ I'm a mem-ber of the coun - try club."

To Coda

I'M GONNA BE SOMEBODY

Words and Music by TRAVIS TRITT
and JILL COLUCCI

Bob-by played his gui-tar on the hard-er side _ of town, _____

where it's hard for a poor boy to find the mon - ey. _

PUT SOME DRIVE IN YOUR COUNTRY

Words and Music by
TRAVIS TRITT

22

HELP ME HOLD ON

Words and Music by TRAVIS TRITT
and PAT TERRY

SIGN OF THE TIMES

Words and Music by
TRAVIS TRITT

SON OF THE NEW SOUTH

Words and Music by TRAVIS TRITT
and LARRY ALDERMAN

41

IF I WERE A DRINKER

Words and Music by ZACK TURNER
and TIM NICHOLS

48

PLATINUM AWARD FOR "COUNTRY CLUB" WITH JIM ED NORMAN (WARNER BROS. RECORDS)

PHOTO BY DON PUTNAM

THE ROAD HOME

Words and Music by JIM McBRIDE
and STEWART HARRIS

Full moon ris - in' o - ver At - lan -
Cat - tails grow - in' down by the riv -

if I don't go back some - day. _____

Hey yeah,

Repeat ad lib. and Fade

DRIFT OFF TO DREAM

Words and Music by TRAVIS TRITT
and STEWART HARRIS

* Rit. on D.S. only

DIXIE FLYER

Words and Music by SUSAN LONGACRE,
JIM PHOTOGLO and RUSSELL SMITH

Well, the first _

_ thing I re - mem - ber _ was _ the smell of burn - in'
first chance I got I _ was gone _ like a
Full speed a - head. No, I _ ain't _ stop - pin'
Some are sat - is - fied _ just to sit on _ the

MCA music publishing

Instrumental ad lib.

Hey, _____
(Vocal 1st time only)

Ride   on _____

Repeat ad lib. and Fade

TRAVIS tritt

IT'S ALL ABOUT TO CHANGE

PHOTO BY PETER NASH

THE WHISKEY AIN'T WORKIN'

Words and Music by RONNY SCAIFE
and MARTY STUART

DON'T GIVE YOUR HEART TO A RAMBLER

Words and Music by
JIMMIE SKINNER

or do ___ an - y - thing ___ to spoil ___ your hap - pi - ness. ___

Instrumental solo ends

So, don't fall in love ___

Well, ___ if I ev -

2. *Instrumental solo*

- er ___ get the blues ___ now, ___ sweet ba -

by, ___

or the lure ___ of the high -

give your heart ___ to a ram - bler, _____ lit-tle girl. ___

Bet - ter not, ___ ba - by. Yeah, _____ don't you

give your heart to a ram - bler, _____ lit - tle girl. ___

ANYMORE

Words and Music by TRAVIS TRITT
and JILL COLUCCI

My tears no long-er wait-ing.____ Oh,_____ my re - sis - tance ain't_ that strong.__

HERE'S A QUARTER
(CALL SOMEONE WHO CARES)

Words and Music by
TRAVIS TRITT

BIBLE BELT

Words and Music by
TRAVIS TRITT

church that I grew up in. _____ She was a
-er I could use ad-vice. _____ I got trou-
hear the news of what they did. _____ No-bod-

look-er from At-lan-ta, led the choir, played pi-an-o, had a
-bles with a man that I know you'll un-der-stand. If you could
y could be-lieve that he left his wife to grieve alone

B

bod-y that was made for sin. _____ She did-n't
help me it would sure be nice." _____ They met a
with two pre-school kids. _____ I don't know

E7

care that he was mar-ried 'cause the torch that she car-ried was hot-
few min-utes af-ter in the of-fice of the pas-tor and she
how they're doin, but I know that they're screwin' up a

102

104

IT'S ALL ABOUT TO CHANGE

Words and Music by
TRAVIS TRITT

NOTHING SHORT OF DYING

Words and Music by
TRAVIS TRITT

IF HELL HAD A JUKEBOX

(Title Suggested by LEE ROGERS)
Words and Music by TRAVIS TRITT

You left ___ me for ___ a dream ___ you had ___ to fol - low.
looked at all ___ the pic - tures from ___ our good ___ times

But I thought good-bye would-n't last ___ that long. ___
and I tried to fig - ure out where we ___ went wrong.

You'd go ___ off chas - ing rain - bows ___ till you
And I've dropped a mil - lion quar - ters down the juke-

SOMEONE FOR ME

Words and Music by TRAVIS TRITT
and STEWART HARRIS

122

PHOTO BY DEAN DIXON

HOMESICK

Words and Music by BUDDY BUIE
and J.R. COBB

Driving Country
no chord

8va bassa 2nd time

Gui- tars ring in the dead of night, ___ sing so blue, ___ sound so right. ___

PHOTO BY DEAN DIXON